# Story Paper

Name

Class

www.ingramcontent.com/pod-product-compliance
Lightning Source LLC
Chambersburg PA
CBHW080601220526
45466CB00010B/3216
* 9 7 8 1 6 5 6 1 9 9 8 2 9 *